The Perfect Place

MESSAGES TO INSPIRE THE CREATIVE HEART

WRITTEN AND ILLUSTRATED BY
WENDY DEWAR HUGHES

MESSAGES TO INSPIRE THE CREATIVE HEART

WRITTEN AND ILLUSTRATED BY
WENDY DEWAR HUGHES

The Perfect Place - Messages to Inspire the Creative Heart

Copyright 2018 © Wendy Dewar Hughes

All rights reserved. Artwork and writing is all original work of Wendy Dewar Hughes. No part of this publication may be reproduced, stored in a retrieval system, or transmitted in any form or by any means – electronic, mechanical, digital, photocopy, recording, or any other – without the prior permission of the author.

www.wendydewarhughes.com
www.summerbaystudio.com

Published by Summer Bay Press.
Agassiz, British Columbia V0M 1A2
www.summerbaypress.com

Editing, Interior Design and Cover Design:
Wendy Dewar Hughes, Summer Bay Press

ISBN: 978-1-927626-82-5

Being creative isn't always easy;
in fact, it is sometimes difficult.
But it is always satisfying.
Keep that in mind.

Today is going to be a great day. Look for the blessings coming your way.

Do something good for yourself today. Buy yourself flowers, take a walk through the park, have a nap. You must take good care of yourself to be creative and productive.

To avoid burnout, take regular mental-health breaks. Read a book, see a movie, meditate or pray, and hang out with happy people.

Unless you're actually at fault and need to apologize, never let a vague feeling of guilt be a motivator.

Take five or ten minutes and learn something new today. Read a book or watch a how-to video on the Internet.

Rather than listening to the radio when you drive, borrow some library books on CD, or download some audio books. You can "read" while you drive.

 Take a stillness break and completely relax every muscle in your body for ten to fifteen minutes a day. Relax your mind, too.

Write a new story of your life, the way you want it to look. Imagine yourself in the lead role and see how you feel.

Stop blaming others for your problems. Instead, look for solutions that you have the power to implement.

Wallowing in blame won't improve your situation. Move on.

Take care of your own needs rather than waiting for someone else to do it. You are responsible for your own happiness.

There is a reason God advises us to forgive. When you do, you will no longer spend energy on carrying that past pain.

Try going to bed when you first feel sleepy, even if it seems too early. Listen to your body and increase your wellness.

Instead of having a to-do list everyday, take a day and have a not-to-do list.

Write down what you decide you don't need to do, ever.

Is your mind cluttered with mental baggage that is weighing you down and sapping your energy? Toss it out and make more free space in your soul.

Do you feel tired when you think about a particular project? Perhaps it is your heart telling you that this project is not for you.

Does perfectionism make you procrastinate? Rather than looking at your project as a whole, try seeing only the next step and take that one.

Unsatisfied needs are good motivators. If you find yourself unmotivated to do something, perhaps you don't need it.

Believe that God is working things out for you even when you can't see it. Just believe.

If something gives you bad
feelings, walk away.
Listen to your intuition.

Just tell the truth. It will simplify your life immeasurably.

Be thankful that you've arrived
at another new day.
God has blessed you indeed.

Live what you love. Whenever you have a choice to make, ask yourself if this is something you truly love.

What you listen to you will eventually believe. Why? Because faith comes by hearing.
Be careful what you listen to because it will change your life, either good or bad.

Don't waste your time living someone else's version of your life.
You don't have time for that.

Let go of comparing yourself
and your work to others'.
Pay attention to your own path.

If you're going to compare, look at how far you've come, not how far you have to go. It's so much more motivating.

God reveals himself to those who want to know him. Just seek him with all your heart.
You'll find him.

When you go after what you really want, you will always be glad you did.

Take time to coast. Full speed ahead all the time is not a sustainable strategy.

Clutter on your desk or work area can create clutter and frustration in your mind. Take some time today to clean or tidy up even a small space.

Pain in your body may be an indication of emotional pain. Your mind and your body are intimately acquainted. Explore unresolved emotional pain and your physical pain may resolve, too.

The busyness of life can easily crowd out the source of life. Spend some time alone with God today.

If you know it's right for you, hold your ground. Listen but don't be swayed by the opinions or advice of others.

When your enthusiasm for everything is running low, it's probably time for a vacation.

Know what gets your juices flowing and build more of those into your daily life. While not everything you do will be a thrill, when you have happy things built in, your energy will go up.

Like it or fix it, don't just complain about it. Complaining about your life has no redeeming virtues and accomplishes nothing.

"Getting things off your chest" often simply dumps them on someone else. Examine what is bothering you and take steps to correct it.

Failure has a way of scaring you off trying new things. Don't let it. Instead, examine how you can do things differently based on what you have learned.

Remember that treating others as you wish to be treated always works. If you want to be treated well, treat others well.

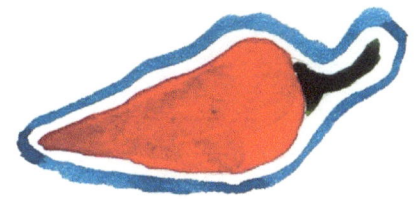

Ask yourself this question:
Is there an easier way to
accomplish this task?
Is there a shorter distance to
getting this done?

Christ said that his yoke was easy and his burden light. If what you're carrying is not easy or light perhaps what you're doing is not from God.

Delegate, off-load, outsource. You don't have to do everything yourself, in fact, trying to do everything yourself can stand in the way of your success.

Every day, do something that moves you toward the your most important goals and dreams. It doesn't matter how small the steps.

You are the only person whose thoughts should occupy your mind. Be careful what you let in.

When you're feeling stressed and alone, nothing works better than prayer. God is waiting for you to ask for help. He won't push it on you.

If you get nervous speaking in front of people, the easiest way to conquer it is to stop thinking about yourself. Become "other" conscious rather than "self" conscious.

To have a friend you must first be a friend. Don't wait for special relationships to come to you. If you want more friends, be friendlier.

No one can read your mind, nor can anyone give you what you want if they don't know what that is.
Ask for what you want.

Here is a simple success formula:
Decide what you want to do.
Write it down. Pray about it.
Do the steps.

Feeling uncreative? Tap into an emotion that you don't normally express in your art or writing. Try expressing it in a different way.

Starting a new project can be difficult without a clear plan. Begin by taking the first small step then follow it with the next one. The path will become clear.

Without a destination you won't know where you're going. Decide where you want to end up then take the steps to get to that destination.

You have to believe in yourself. What you say about yourself has power.

Take the word "try" out of your vocabulary. Try doesn't do anything. Where there is no action, nothing gets done.

Stop saying you can't do something. Either you want to and you will go ahead and do it, or you don't want to and you won't.

Simply hoping something will happen will keep you stuck. Take action, or don't take action. Don't sit and just hope something will happen.

Your language is part of your success. Change how you talk about yourself and what you want and you will change your outcomes.

Everyone is potentially worth your time. Who knows where each connection may lead?

*You only have one life here so make the most of it.
Be happy.*

Having only a hazy idea of what you want to achieve won't take you there. Clear away the fog and make a plan.

Calm yourself. If your mind is buzzing with thoughts and ideas, write them down in your journal, or on sticky notes that you can post where you can see them.

Notice the little luxuries in your life today. Good coffee, fresh flowers, a nice piece of jewelry or clothing to wear. Luxury is all around you.

Spend a day meandering.
Take your camera, sketchbook,
or journal and record your
journey to nowhere in particular.

"But that will take so much time," you protest. You're going to spend the time anyway. You might as well spend it going after your dreams.

Self-pity will open the door to all kinds of negative thoughts. Refuse to be pitiful and close that door before your mind is invaded.

Sometimes things don't work out exactly as you've planned but if you don't give up, something will work out. Maybe God has something even better in store for you.

Feeling alone and being alone is not the same thing. If you're feeling alone, find someone to talk to, and if you are alone and would rather not be, find someone to be with.

Work at your craft without judgment until you have finished. Everything can look bad in the middle but can turn out wonderfully in the end.

Those who are the most blessed by God are those who seek his presence the most. When you search for him, you will find him.

Trying to be all things to all people means being very little to everyone. Focus on your true calling and you will be there for the people who really need you.

Time may not heal a broken heart but God will. Jesus came to bind up broken hearts and he still does.

"It came to pass" is a good reminder to keep your perspective. Few things are permanent.

What others think of you is not your business. Instead, concentrate on what you think of yourself and let others think whatever they want.

Let go of hurts, slights, rudeness, and insults. They only have something to do with you if you take them on.

Life's obstacles may slow you down a bit but they don't have to stop you. Don't let them.

If you find yourself passing up opportunities for no good reason you may be unconsciously sabotaging yourself. Take some time to explore what's behind your resistance.

Give yourself permission not to be perfect. Allow yourself to do bad work. Take the pressure off and see what happens.

Identify what success looks like to you. Say it out loud and writing it down. See how it helps you focus.

Get good at whatever you want to do. Find creative ways to follow your calling.

If people close to you sabotage your creative efforts, remember that no one can stop your without your consent.

Time and space are necessary for the creative person. Build them into your life or you will soon be starved for creative outlets.

Throw yourself into what you love to do. You'll be happier for it.

Attend events and conferences on the subject of your passion. This is where you find your tribe.

The people who tell you that what you want to do is impossible will probably never attempt it themselves anyway. Why listen to them?

The safe, comfortable answer may not be the right answer. To dramatically change your life, you may have to do something dramatically different.

Everything you do starts with a thought. Decide which thoughts you want to expand on and go from there.

Worry is the biggest waste of time there is. It accomplishes nothing and destroys your peace. Stop worrying and trust God.

Other Books by Wendy Dewar Hughes

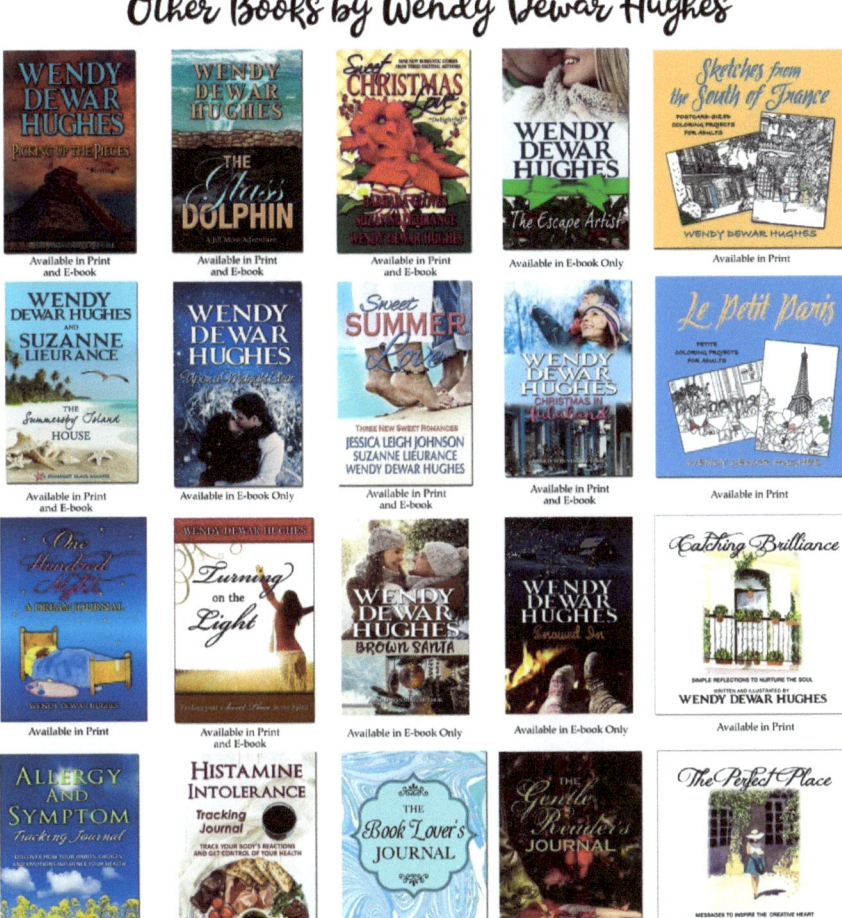

And more coming soon to online booksellers.

www.ingramcontent.com/pod-product-compliance
Lightning Source LLC
Chambersburg PA
CBHW042036150426
43201CB00003B/40